Alaska Our Way

Donna

Hope you enjoy!

Elaine Held

Alaska Our Way

Elaine Brooks Held

Library of Congress Control Number:		2012909330
ISBN:	Hardcover	978-1-4771-1784-2
	Softcover	978-1-4771-1783-5
	Ebook	978-1-4771-1785-9

This book was printed in the United States of America.

To order additional copies of this book, contact:
Xlibris Corporation
1-888-795-4274
www.Xlibris.com
Orders@Xlibris.com
112900

CONTENTS

Eagles sliced slits in the morning mist,
the cuts trailing cotton candy strands.

THE FOLLOWING ARE SHORT STORIES
I CALL SNIPPETS OF OUR EXPERIENCES
TRAVELING TO AND IN ALASKA.

THE DREADED CANADIAN BORDER

1997-2011

T HE ONLY TIME we have crossed the Canadian border without incident was the year after 9/11.

The first year we crossed, we were too innocent to understand there was a problem, with the border personnel wearing bulletproof vests. We would only find out later that the United States and British Columbia of Canada were coming to blows over salmon. It was that year some fishermen took an American ferry and its passengers hostage—an international offense. It was our first trip, so we excitedly pulled up to the booth. I noticed an instant change in the demeanor of the person who approached us as soon as she saw our California license. Instead of the usual questions, she asked, "Do you have any weapons?" When she seemed satisfied that we indeed did not have an uzzy with us, she asked us to pull over to a large open area. Should we be worried? Two scowling men approached. "Get out of the motor home. Take any valuables with you. Stand to the side." I looked at Bill. I thought to myself, *I think I am going to lose the apples in the refrigerator.* Then the seriousness of the situation hit me as I remembered I had a needle with a strange-looking substance for seasickness in the refrigerator. Sweating, I couldn't look at Bill. I was going to spend the rest of my life in a Canadian jail.

One of the men was trying to lift our ice chest out of the shower and was having a difficult time. Not thinking, Bill stepped on the bottom step to help. The man whirled on him, shouting, "Do not come in here. I told you that!" *Oh boy, we are dead.* Suddenly, they were finished and told us to get in and leave. We didn't argue. After we were a good way from the border, we began to shake. I told Bill about the needle. That was when we pulled over, and Bill opened the fridge door. The needle had slipped behind a package of cheese not to be seen.

The next year, we were old hands at this crossing business. We were with our friends Johnny and Sharon, who were newcomers. Again, we were pulled over. The man asked Bill for our poultry. *Poultry! You want our chicken? Huh!* I had forgotten about the bird flu in LA. We only had three dozen eggs, so we gave it to him. We were sent on, and we stopped to go back and help Sharon. Sharon, being the nice person she is, did not think to hide anything. She told him she had frozen chicken and canned turkey, so he took that along with her eggs. For some reason, he wanted to see the dry dog food and sure enough that had chicken in it, so off it went. That was too much for Sharon. Chicken by-products in dry dog food made on the East Coast? Poor Trouffles would not have his special diet all across Canada. The Americans on the other side were taking all the beef because of the mad cow thing. We were giving them a bad time about eating well. One side fixed breakfast and the other dinner.

Another year, we were traveling with Don and Mary, and again we were pulled over. Two women were going through our rig with white gloves. One of them opened the drawer below the fridge and took out a large perforated spoon. She looked at it like it was party to some crime, so I offered my help by explaining it was my cat's pooper scooper. That was the end of that exam.

One year, on the way home, we had a refrigerator full of frozen salmon. Bill had taken the rubber gasket off the freezer and allowed the whole thing to freeze. Then he covered the area with hard foam and secured all of this with duct tape. We arrived at the American border, and of course, they pulled us over. The man came in the RV and asked if we had any meat products. We told him about the salmon. Instantly, he looked into the fridge and turned with a perplexed look. We explained, and he said he had to see the inside. When he started to undo all the wrapping, he gave up and sent us on our way.

CANADA

I STOOD ON the edge of a small town in western Canada taking in the cool, crisp early-spring air. Coming up behind me was a sound so out of place I had to turn and face it. Stunned, I could only gape. A worn young man on horseback brushed by me. Slightly behind the horse was a dun-colored mangy dog obviously not bothered by hard travel. A town dog began to yap at the trio. The horse knew better than to alter his gait, and the dog couldn't be bothered by such a useless, pampered thing. Only the young man turned his lean, hard body, allowing me a glimpse of clear blue eyes. His clothes were of another era, a rifle tight to the worn saddle. What in his past led him to value his present companions over a convertible and other young men his age? Wondering, I watched as they moved off in a tight unit to welcome the wilderness.

Mosquito netting

W E WEREN'T PREPARED for the mosquitoes. I bought a bug jacket that looks like a hazmat suit. Bill was up all night fighting mosquitoes, so he duct-taped everything—the windows, vents, everything. Our RV is very old, so everybody assumes the duct tape is holding the RV together. Now the only thing that can get in the RV is the mosquitoes.

Before the ferry, we were going to spend the night in a pull out. We just got stopped when two Mounties in a pickup pulled in and came up to us. They told us not to spend the night there. Someone had hit and killed a bear cub up the road a hundred yards, and the mother bear wouldn't leave.

When they picked up the body, they had to fire their shotgun in the air to keep her from charging them. We got the heck out of there.

We crossed on a ferry to get to Yellowknife. The lake was still frozen with a thin cover. The ice scraping on each side was so loud I couldn't talk on the video camera. It was very unnerving, and then the man who ran the ferry gave me a warning to read. He laughed when he saw the look on my face and then said, "That is just in case we have to jump overboard." When he stopped laughing, he told me that was his private joke for Californians. There were many native people on the ferry, and they were doubled up laughing at me, so I joined them.

Mud

After leaving Yellowknife, there was twenty miles of muddy construction and had covered the entire RV. We couldn't see out the back or side windows. It was raining so hard Bill was fooling with the windshield wipers, and the horn went off. It scared us both, but we managed a laugh. We crossed on the same ferry. It was so windy the water was blasting over the front of the ferry. We were the first ones, so we had a free RV wash. The lake was so rough it was splashing the front of the RV up to the windows.

On the way to Fort Simpson, we raced a mallard duck for quite a ways at 35 mph. The duck won when Bill had to slow down for a pothole.

We stopped to talk to a couple who had pioneered in that area a long time ago. They were in their seventies now. They told us that in the beginning they had built their own house and gathered their own food. They lived by the river, and that was their only transportation. His hands were a mess from old frostbite. They had wonderful stories to tell. She had chickens now and knew them all by name. "Only the useless roosters are cooked and eaten," she told me, laughing.

HAZELTON

All of Hazelton helping

L EAVING THE TOWN of Hazelton, Bill noticed something wrong
with the RV. He couldn't figure it out, but about then, the back
axle froze. We made it into the town of New Hazelton, which is about four
blocks long. There was a post office with a parking lot, and Bill made it
that far. Don and Mary followed us. This area of Canada was all logging
before the mills shut down. Many men were out of work.

Within an hour, there were thirty pickup trucks in and around the
parking lot with us as the center of attraction. They all assessed the situation
and got the RV up on blocks, ready to do whatever was needed. Billy went
to his dad's and got a welder to help release the axle. It took some doing,

but they managed it. These guys worked on their logging trucks all the time and knew what they were doing.

Now we needed a new hub. Billy's girlfriend Jennifer worked at NAPA and tried to find one, but there wasn't anything to be had. It was now time to call it a day. Billy told us his dad owned the only restaurant in town, and he made sure we had dinner there. When we opened the door, everybody there knew our story. They were shouting things like "Kidnap the Americans until their president helps our logging." We spent two hours of hilarity.

The next day, Bobby took Bill all over to try and find a hub. They went to all the dumps and any place else Bobby could think of. Finally, Bobby said, "This is stupid. Listen, see that RV across the street in my yard? Obviously, it is not going anywhere this summer. I'm going to take the hub off of mine and put it on yours, and you can bring me a new one when you come through." Billy, Bobby, and Shane were now family and have been ever since. Thanks, guys!

FERRIES

Disappearing into Alaskan Ferry

B ILL AND I used the ferry system to get around the Inland Passage with our RV in 1997. Our first time on the ferry was quite an experience. They put us in line according to where we were getting off. The rigs that were getting off last got on first. We watched carefully as the line disappeared like Jonah into the whale. Soon it was our turn. We inched our way along until we got to the ramp. I gasped. It seemed to go straight down. I was so intent on the ramp that when I raised my vision, I yelled. I scared Bill so vividly he slammed on the brakes, yelling, "What's the matter?" All I could do was point.

Bill looked up and mirrored my panic. It looked as if we could easily go right on through into the water as the big door on the other side was open.

Bill eased the RV onto the ferry. The man directing people into the ferry was rolling his eyes and frantically motioning for us to hurry up. We were holding up the line. He walked up to Bill's window and said sarcastically, "First time?" Our wide eyes answered. "Well, sir," he continued, getting in Bill's face, "I want you to listen to me carefully. I am going to walk over there in front of you. I am going to direct you. Do not look at your wife! Do not take your eyes off of me. Do you understand?"

Bill sheepishly nodded. The man moved away from us walking backward as if he expected us to run over him. He motioned for Bill to drive forward. Bill automatically turned and looked at me.

The man started screaming, "No! No! No! Do not look at your wife! Do not take your eyes off of me! Now, let's try this again."

Bill was so embarrassed it took him a month before he would look at me. Now that he had the routine down, we followed the man. He parked us so you couldn't get a piece of paper between us and the rig in front and the rig on the side. We had packed a backpack and a blanket. We exited and followed a person that was motioning us to the stairway. The passenger deck opened up with beautiful windows on three sides. Comfortable seats like airplane seats were available. The trip was a highlight. Whales, eagles, and Dahl porpoises were pointed out by a naturalist. When it was time to exit at Ketchikan, Bill was acting like a seasoned ferry passenger and buzzed right off and up the ramp.

FULL FERRY

E VEN THOUGH YOU had a reservation, sometimes all the pieces of the puzzle didn't fit, and one or two rigs had to stay behind and wait for the next ferry. On one trip, we knew we were in trouble by the number of vehicles waiting in line in front of us. We were one of the last ones to get there, so we were at the end of the line.

Two Australian girls we had become friends with were the only ones behind us. Marie talked to Bill while we waited nervously. Finally, our line moved up as everyone else was on. When we got to the ramp, the woman there informed us we would probably have to stay behind. Then we were eased on. Another rig had left to be with their traveling companions, and that left room for us. The ferry was so full they were putting us in front sideways. The far door was closed.

Now to get Marie on, they had all the rigs move forward, the front ones pushing against the door. Marie drove on, but the width of her bumper hung over. We all drove hard forward against each other while Marie accelerated. They closed the door behind her, scraping her bumper. The captain was informed he would have to dock turned around because we wouldn't be able to back out.

When we got to the next town, they opened the doors on the opposite side, and vehicles just drove off except for one little truck and camper. We wondered what was going on, and later were told the only way they could get him on was to have him squeeze into a kitty-corner space. To get him off, they had to have him back up so all of the truck back of the tires was hanging over the water. They offered to drive the truck for him, and the couple gratefully jumped out and watched. Well, the husband watched while his wife turned her back and covered her eyes.

PETS ON A FERRY

T HOSE WHO HAD pets had to leave them in the rigs, and no one was allowed below. Once an hour, they made an announcement, and those with pets were allowed to go below and check on them. A woman with a dog had brought along a small blue tarp she could spread on the deck for her dog to do what he needed. Her dog was gratefully using the tarp when suddenly there was a loud commotion. There were several dogs whose owners were dragging them to the blue tarp. They were all apologizing to the startled woman and offering to clean the tarp. It looked like a doggy run on a cruise ship. The fourteen dogs using it were very attentively ignoring one another with as much dignity as they could.

KODIAK FERRY

B EAUTIFUL HOMER LAY on a spit in the bay. We watched from the dock as the approaching ferry appeared in front of the majestic mountains surrounding the bay. Even as experienced as we were, we could not contain our excitement going on this ferry to Kodiak. Don and Mary were going with us in our twenty-one-foot RV.

We watched the ferry come around the end of the spit and then looked back at the dock. What was this? There was no place on the dock that had a ramp that would take us below into the ferry. How were we going to get aboard? The ferry eased in, and the small line moved up. I got out to videotape the process, and then I saw what was happening. I ran back to Bill and shouted, "Bill! You're going onto an elevator." I got the look, so I left him to find out for himself.

As he approached, I filmed. He was directed onto a flat elevator just large enough for a large RV. When on, they blocked the wheels and lowered him into the bottom of the ferry. At the bottom, the elevator rotated, and he drove off. Simple. Don and Mary had walked on to save us the best chairs for the long, bumpy ride.

TUNDRA

Tundra in the Fall

S TANDING ON THE springy surface of the tundra that stretches hundreds of miles in every direction is like standing on the surface of another planet. The wind blows hard enough to bend you over. Rolling mountains as far as you can see give me the feeling of wilderness for the first time. The millions of wee flowers and plants give off a scent you won't find anywhere else in the world.

We are the only vehicle on the Rim of the World Highway. Looking into the distance, the undulating tundra looks green, but if you get down on your hands and knees and look, you will be surprised. The desolate-looking surface is full of life and all the colors of the rainbow. Most of the plant life is rich in nutrition. The caribou thrive on it. It was not meant for human habitation, and maybe God meant it that way to protect the wild. But there is something that draws you in.

The space is too big, so big it is uncomfortable. The few trees that try to grow were called little sticks by the Russians. The trees that grow are about three feet high and are literally sticks. There is not enough topsoil for them to do anything else. The roots have nothing to hold on to, so many lean until they fall. There is nothing to break the monotony of rounded shades of green meeting the sky. Nothing to break the wind. A single piece of paper blown from a passing vehicle flutters and flies in unbroken space. I watch it fly unheeded to the horizon, the only nongreen matter.

CHICKEN, ALASKA

ON A WET gray day, we traveled down a narrow two-lane asphalt road to reach Chicken. We came over a rise to see the last of our paved road disappear into a gravel ribbon stretching to the horizon. The only rest area was on our right, but Bill came to a complete stop on the road instead of turning in.

There was an airplane taking up the rest stop. Bill eased in beside it and got out to ask the man getting into the plane if we were in his way. "No," he answered. "Just needed to make a pit stop." And off he went down the road, lifting off into the sky. By this time, nothing an Alaskan did surprised us.

It was a long one hundred miles on gravel to get there, but coming around a bend, we saw below us a building with a huge sign on the roof that said Chicken. It needed it so strangers could find it, I guess, since that was virtually the only building in town.

Chicken, Alaska, is one of the remotest but most interesting towns in Alaska. There were people still mining for a living. There were only six people living in the town itself. You would think they would be close friends, but not so. The woman who owned the town bought it about ten years ago. Another family bought the tiny store and bar from her. When AAA came in to ask what Chicken had to offer to put it in the AAA book, the renter told them it was her town and she led the tours. That started the feud. That was how the woman who owned the town made her living.

The book *Tisha* takes place in Chicken, and Tisha's daughter sits on the front porch of the woman who owns the town and signs the book for tourists. The town is called Chicken because the early miners wanted to call it Ptarmigan, an Alaskan bird, but couldn't spell it so, therefore, Chicken.

Chicken

Bill and I had to go into the famous little bar for one drink. As soon I walked in, I began to laugh. The man behind the bar had on a Spam shirt. Since I am from Austin, Minnesota, which is known as Spam Town, I knew about the shirt. We had our picture taken together in our identical Spam shirts. We since have become good friends, and we visit every year.

We had just gotten our mail, and in it was a jury summons. We had it postmarked Chicken, Alaska, and sent it back. We haven't been called since.

SEWARD

S EWARD IS A beautiful bay with eagles, otters, and cruise ships that rest quietly. Even most of the fishing is done by boat. We walked down to the fish cleaning area to watch when the charter boats came in. The fish are weighed and the people can have their picture taken with the huge fish. Then the charter fishermen clean the fish.

One lady named Spook is heavyset and about fifty with one spin-and-glow earring and one lure earring and a fish necklace. Boy is she good at cleaning fish. All the men defer to her as she was the one who taught them all. She has invented the cleaning knives and the sharpener that all the men use. She constantly talks while she is cleaning. She will find some kids, and she will have them come over, and she will tell them about the fish.

One kid asked her why she did this for a living because she was a woman. Spook took a while and then said, "Somebody has to be a friend to the fish." The kid thought about it and then told her that cleaning fish wasn't being good to the fish, and she answered, "It is if you are good at it. And I like to fish, so why shouldn't I do it?" The kid told her she was good even if she was a girl.

The young men working with her sometimes make a bad cut, and she will go over and show them. She watches them carefully. It is free entertainment, especially when the young men get to kidding and teasing one another. Parents then usher their kids to the ice-cream parlor!

HOMER

Homer spit

H OMER IS SITUATED in the most beautiful setting I have ever seen. The town is nestled on the northern edge of a crystal blue bay that you view from above. The bay opens up to the Inland Passage on the southwest corner. The RV parks and saltwater fishing businesses are located on an incredible spit that breaks the bay almost entirely in half. Eagles are abundant because in the winter a lonely widow spends her entire pension on meat to feed the eagles. She spends all her time cutting the meat up and putting it into ice chests that fill the back of her old, beat-up, rusty station wagon. She slowly creeps through the ice and snow of winter until she reaches the spit. Eagles begin to soar over the spot for they know what is coming and trust the old woman. She takes one ice chest at a time and unloads the meat on the snow. Before she can leave the area to get a second chest, the eagles are flaring and landing. There is a picture of her amid three hundred eagles. She is standing with her arms raised, greeting the flaring eagles with only snow and vivid blue water as a frame.

Woman feeding Eagles

SITKA

BEAUTIFUL SITKA CAN only be reached by boat or plane. We arrived late after little sleep. In the ferry parking lot, a limo with the driver in outfit waited for someone to get off the ferry. Another man in uniform walked up, leading a full-size black poodle with all the necessary jewelry. The chauffer opened the limo door, and the huge dog daintily entered. They sped off into what most people would call a wilderness.

We found our RV park, and friends found us. Bill had gotten out to crush cans, and two men came running, shouting, "Bill, where are you?" By this time, everybody knew the sound of Bill crushing cans. The men decided to hire a fishing boat for the following day. When Bill returned, all he could talk about was the stories the young man piloting the boat had told him. Two of the stories went like this.

Dave and a good friend went moose hunting. They did not see an animal the entire four days. Giving up, they got in their rusted Alaskan truck and were driving back to Sitka when they saw a German tourist bus stopped by the side of the road. All the people were out lined up taking pictures of something. Dave looked at his friend and said, "You don't suppose?" His friend replied, "Now, Dave, just drive on by. Don't even think of it." Sure enough, the entire German contingency was standing on one side of the road, and a huge moose stood on the other. Yes, Dave pulled over and shot the moose in front of everyone. "You would have thought it was Bambi," mused Dave.

Dave's friend Hank flew helicopters for his lumber business in Sitka. There was no dock in Sitka, so cruise ship tourists took little shuttles back and forth to the big ship. One day, Hank filled his copter with old tires and gasoline and flew to the nearby volcanic island. There he dumped the tires in the opening of the extinct volcano and lit them. Smoke billowed. The cruise ship frantically tried to start their huge engines and get them powered up while trying to get all their passengers back on board. The citizens of Sitka ran for their light planes and fishing boats to escape the volcano's wrath. Emergency organizations went into full red alert. It was hours before anyone found out it was an April Fool's hoax.

The next day, we were eating breakfast in our RV and listening to the local radio station. There was world news, and we hadn't heard any news for a month. All of a sudden the sound went off. We listened, waiting, but it took a while before they came back on. When they did, a man made an announcement that they had so many complaints about playing yesterday's news they would now go to music. After a while, the local news came on with a man in a helicopter above us giving the morning traffic report. "There is one car in the bakery parking lot and one car on Highway 1. Go to the bakery, and you will be put into the drawing for a ride with me tomorrow for the traffic report." Coming from LA, we laughed until we were sick.

KENAI

Kenai Sunset

CAMPED ON A bluff overlooking the Kenai, oranges and reds flooded the sky. Since the sun doesn't set all the way, a sunset lasts for hours. Inside the motor home, every item was tinged with a brilliant red. Standing on the bluff, various bird songs invaded the silence as I took in the wild smells of Alaska. Below me, Don and Bill walked a wide flat beach. The river reflected red with black boat dots marring the surface. Three snow-covered peaks thrust into the redness directly across from me. Iliamna. How could an English word be better than that soft Indian name? Iliamna. Perfect sound for a mountain that can restore your soul.

PRINCE OF WALES ISLAND

Prince of Wales Old growth

THE ISLAND IS remote, and the only work is logging. Two little towns are the only spots of civilization on the immense island. Old growth is abundant. We stopped on a narrow road next to a river so Don, Bill, and I could fish in the rain. We had to crawl over and under huge downed old-growth trees where the rain didn't reach us.

An Alaskan family was camped near the river in a tent. None of them wore rain gear or shoes. They were sopping wet, their tent was wet, their food was wet, but they didn't even seem to notice. When we walked to the river, their two boys, ages eight and ten, joined us. They didn't get much chance to talk to cheechakos, or outsiders. The boy talking to Bill told him they lived in a house on a raft in a bay, and when they got tired of that bay, they had it pulled to another bay. They had no electricity or running water. Bill asked him if he had any other siblings. He said yes, but his older brother was a city slicker. He lived in Craig, a town of three thousand on the island. The boy talking to me asked where I lived. I answered, "Los Angeles, California." He didn't know where that was. He asked, "Do you live near the forest?"

"If you drive one hundred miles."

"Gee gosh!" he said. "I don't want to live there."

We found out everybody on the island knew everybody else. The two boys were known, and five years later when we were talking to an Alaskan from the island who was wintering in Quartzsite, he said he knew the boys and filled us in on the latest.

Don, Mary, Bill, and I spent ten days in the wilderness on the island. It was old world damp with a darkness that was protectively soothing. We had mostly fish to eat and worked at keeping the inside of the RV dry. We traveled the narrow logging roads on Sunday so we didn't have to worry about the logging trucks barreling into us. When we surfaced at Craig, we headed for the only store on the island. Four bodies headed straight for the ice-cream freezer. Don bought a square box of mint chocolate ice cream, and we headed for the RV. Without a word, Don got out his machete and cut the rectangular box into fourths, and we lit into the delicious green mass. Since then, ice-cream dinner has become a ritual reserved for special occasions.

DENALI

Denali

F EET ON A rail, we ate with our plates of steak and asparagus on our laps. The gentle refrains of John Denver dissipated around us. Eagles soared overhead, following the river that wound below us. Sharp, crisp, brilliant images of Denali were framed by trees and clouds. The setting sun was coloring the pointed, snow-capped dome pink. As each overlapped lower peak was hit by the light, it changed color, slowly fading into gray.

The four of us took the bus tour through Denali. The day was perfect for seeing the park. The mountain was out, and the sky was clear. We had gone in quite a ways before we sighted any wildlife, but once we did—wow!

We saw thirteen grizzlies, a moose, a fox, and a sheep. When I say thirteen grizzlies, I am not talking about sighting a moving object a mile away. No, in fact, we weren't sure how safe the bus was to protect us from the bears scratching their heinies on the side.

The first bunch of bears crossed the road right in front of the bus. The bus must have looked strange to the bears with sides that had moving things sticking out. We all fought for windows to videotape the spectacle. One of the bears decided to use the road and walked slowly in front of us. Since you are not allowed to startle the bears, we had to crawl along behind her. The bus driver had to keep to a schedule, so he called in to ask permission to use his air brakes to scare her. When the air made a loud noise, she turned around and gave the bus a dirty look and kept going. They told the bus driver to try his horn. She stopped and glared at us. *Okay! The road is yours to do with as you please.* The next bear was walking to the side of the road moving in the same direction the bus was going. Coming in the opposite direction on the opposite side of the road was a happy-go-lucky fox. He hopped and played and actually looked like he was smiling. The bus driver stopped the bus.

"Uh-oh. Folks, we may be witnesses to the food chain. You might want to turn away."

There was no way anybody was going to miss whatever was about to happen. The fox was hopping until he got right across from the bear. On one of his hops, he got a good look at what was ten feet from him. It looked exactly like a cartoon. The fox went straight up, his legs digging for traction. All you could see was dirt flying. Then his feet got a hold, and he screamed up the little hill. He stopped on a rock and stretched to watch the bear who couldn't have cared less. She was too busy eating berries at the moment, thank you.

SUTTON

OUTSIDE OF SUTTON, there is a huge area where people may camp and ride. We like to ride up to the old coal mine and look for fossils. The area of the mine is cut out in layers like huge steps.

I had crawled up to the top layer to get a good look and take pictures. As I crawled over the edge, there was a tall berm I needed to go over. I was in the act of crawling over when I let myself drop to the flat. A young moose thought he was all alone up there, and I scared him so bad he tried to jump over the bluff but realized at the last moment that was not a good decision. He leaped up and over a ten-foot bank and was gone. I don't know who scared who more!

FAIRBANKS

Roadkill and Don

OVER THE CB, Don yelled, "Roadkill! Roadkill!" And he yanked his fifth wheel over to the side of the road, causing it to bounce and roll. Bill answered, "Oh boy!" And we were also yanked to the side. They ran around gathering saws, pliers, hammers, gloves, and anything else they needed. By this time, Mary and I knew the routine, so we busied ourselves taking pictures. When they had all the bones they wanted, we were on our way again.

We pulled into Fairbanks and settled into our spot at the RV campground. Mary and I bustled around getting everything ready to start dinner. Don and Bill got out their makeshift boiling pots since Mary and

I would not let them use our good ones. They threw in the bones they had found to boil off all the gunk. Mary and I decided to delay dinner. Walking around the campground, we were investigating the restrooms when we overheard two women talking.

"What is that nauseating smell?"

"I don't know, but I hope it isn't someone's dinner," the other answered.

Mary and I began to hold our nose as if we didn't know what caused the horrible smell. When the two women trudged off looking for the cause of the odor, we walked across the street to Fred Meyers, distancing ourselves from our husbands.

VALDEZ

IT IS RAINING as we fish. The mist shades each layer of mountain a lighter gray. White mist outlines the ridges, setting off the striated green of the mountains three hundred and sixty degrees around us. Colors of the rainbow outline shafts of light that come through the thinner clouds. The only sound is the piddling of the rain on my hood and the waves of the tide. This will be a hot chocolate night.

KODIAK ISLAND

THE MOON AND sun made a ribbon of the river, highlighting its twists and turns on its way to the saltwater bay. Solitary fishermen dotted the river's edge, their shadows long in the eerie midnight light. Splitting the horizon, a cowboy charged at us, shouting, "Everybody out of the water!" Before we could get over our amazement, he was gone. We began to slowly sidle out but stopped, slack jawed. Dust was beginning to billow and puff on the other side of the rise. What was coming at us? Cattle on Kodiak? Next, humpbacks began undulating, counterpointing to one another. Finally, the whole animal flowed over the rise. Buffalo! Well-seasoned cowboys worked the herd through the river and up the beach, setting it to bobbing and weaving. The flood narrowed to accommodate a gravel road, and they were gone. Slowly, all heads turned to one another, questioning what we had just seen.

KODIAK BEAR

DON, MARY, BILL, and I were driving down a road east of the town of Kodiak. We noticed a traffic jam up ahead. As we eased up behind them, we realized there was no accident. All vehicle occupants were staring and pointing to the side of the road. There was a slight ditch with a twelve-foot cliff leading to heavy trees and undergrowth.

Four pairs of eyes focused on the area, but we could see nothing. Finally, Don said, "I see movement." He told us exactly where to look. Sure enough, something was swinging back and forth just beyond the first canopy of leaves. It was there I made out a round ball of brown fluff. "A baby bear!" We made out two other small cute cubs. The naughty cub had his claws hooked on the bottom branch of a tree and was swinging as a child would. Each time, he would bop his mother on the head. Patiently she stood the onslaught until, just as a human parent would, she roared, "That is enough!" She didn't hit the cub; she hit the tree. A brown fluffy ball rolled over and over. He got up and shook himself. She called him, and he came forgiven.

Two young women in a pickup behind us threw a large handful of roe into the ditch. They hoped the mother bear would leave cover to get the tempting food. Slowly, a massive head raised. A chorus of whoos erupted. The head was a good three feet across. She unfolded and stood shaking her cubs off. Unmoved by the near audience, she moved down the cliff. Her silky caramel-colored fur flowed as she moved closer. She was graceful inside of all that huge muscle mass. We held our breath. Just as she reached the roe, an unsuspecting driver of a small pickup passed everybody on the right. The massive Kodiak bear gave a fake charge, and cars scattered in every direction. A motor home does not do well from zero to sixty, but it tried. It made no difference. We had a flat tire. Bravely, Don and Bill hurried to change it. They could afford to. They set Mary and me up as bait on the road for bear watch.

MIDNIGHT FISHING

THROUGH THE MIDNIGHT half-light, the tall swaying grass lining the river reflected eerily. The wide, flat bank was flopping with sixteen dollies I had just caught. A loud rustling in the grass caused Bill and me to freeze. We sniffed the air for bear. Four ghost-white horses trotted by, and we relaxed.

Don joined us. "I thought the bank was alive, so I got dressed to come out and see what you two were up to." We fished until they quit biting, always listening for bear sounds.

The next night, we stayed in a state campground, canning the dollies late into the night. The following morning, a ranger knocked on our door. "Have you folks seen a bear?"

Bill answered, "No, why?"

"A big one went through the Coast Guard housing, and he was seen in here last night. We have to find him fast and destroy him before he comes back into the residential area."

The motor home became dead silent. Mary turned to me and said, "And we were canning fish half the night?"

We had breakfast and left turning out of our spot. Thirty yards ahead, a large dark shape darted across the road. We discussed what we had seen but weren't sure if it had been a bear. A little beyond where we had seen the shadow was the dump, so Bill pulled in. Thinking of my job, I jumped out and ran around to the other side. Bill was standing stalk still. Immediately freezing, I looked around. The foliage had been smashed flat. The four of us canvassed the area carefully. The large garbage bin had huge bear-proof locks on it. The Kodiak bear had been so powerful he had somehow bent the metal up, rounding it to fit his head. Long cinnamon fur was caught on the metal. We decided discretion was the better part of valor and left.

The next winter, we went to a Fred Hall's Fishing Show in Los Angeles and talked to some men from Kodiak. We related this story, and they said the Coast Guard found the bear and it took sixteen shots to bring the bear down.

CLAMMING

Don clamming results sliced fingers

IN 1999, MY husband and I traveled to Alaska with our friends Don and Mary. When the tides were low, we headed for Clam Gulch to try our luck. You look for the clam's telltale hole, then dig like mad to grab his shell before he outdigs you. The result is fingers and fingernails cut to shreds.

I came up with the brilliant idea of covering my fingers with clear fingernail polish. Don wandered over and asked, "What are you doing?" I explained my theory. "That sounds like it might work. Let me try some." Since Don's fingers were the worst, he slathered it on. Proud of the results, he lifted his hands for me to see. Slowly, a horrified look came over his face. Concerned, I asked, "What's wrong?" He wailed, "I have to go to the bathroom!"

We were in Clam Gulch. Bill and I walked down to the beach first thing. It was cold and misting. There was a storm coming in. The beach was backed by a bluff about forty yards from the water. Across the inlet there were snow-topped mountains. One, Iliamna, was the most beautiful thing I had seen. The water was cold and gray with whitecaps topping the waves. Men in boats got out to bring in the fish caught in their nets. Teddy, dressed in a yellow slicker from head to toe, promised us the flounder that got caught in their nets.

Illiamna

The storm was introduced by long slender black storm clouds that were trailing over the bluffs. Two eagles started at the north end of the inlet and soared all the way down, then turned around and worked hard to get at the head and then did it all over again. The air was so cool and fresh it hurt to breath.

There were families living for the summer at the base of the bluffs. Small children played until it was time to empty the nets. Then they all helped. Once the fish were in, they all piled in the back of an old rusty pickup and charged up the hill to take the fish to a canner. Then back down the road and they were ready for the next run. The kids learned to drive on the beach as soon as they could reach the pedals.

We were camped on the bluff overlooking all of this. We had to be careful because there was a bear cub in the tall grass next to us. We didn't want to excite him. We had an awning between our rigs and a table set up underneath. When we clammed in the morning, we brought them right up the hill and started to clean them. There would be a fire going, and one of us would tend the fire. As soon as the clams opened up, that person dumped them into a container of cold water on another table, and three of us started the assembly line of cleaning. When cleaned, we would either smoke them, grind them up for clam chowder, or leave them the way they were. The final step was to can them. They would be enjoyed for many months during the winter, but not by me.

Don Mary and I cleaning 240 clams

How to lose weight the Alaskan way? Walk down a steep road carrying a bucket and a shovel, then walk down the beach a mile. Dig sixty large clams and carry them back full of water the mile and then up the steep hill. Leave them and take an empty bucket back down the hill, the mile and take some of Bill's clams and repeat. Mary and I found a way to cheat this process. We would stand on the beach making sure to look old and very tired until someone in a truck would tell us to get on the back for a ride. Then clean clam poop for two hours. Or what did you do on your vacation, Elaine?

On our second day of clamming, we met some wonderful, crazy people from Michigan who had a truck. Ah, no carrying up the hill. We went down the beach five miles where the big ones lived. Tomorrow we would go in the opposite direction on the beach. Over the fourth, there would be twenty thousand people joining us for clamming. What a time.

Riding back from the beach, Don had too many clams, and there was a wader in the back of the truck because it was full of water and mud. Don put his extra clams in the wader and even some down the front of his chest waders. John was driving; a lady we had just met and I were in the front. In the back were Don, Bill, Marilyn, and Tom. Tom yelled at John to stop, which he did. Tom explained that there was some homemade wine on the floor behind John. That came out fast, and everybody but the new lady and I had a swig. About another two hundred yards, we came to another screeching halt. This time the new lady had her share. Off we went, and this stopping was repeated several times.

When we pulled up to our campsite, Mary stood waiting with a strange look on her face. Everybody in the back piled out, dropping to the ground and staying there. The lady we had just met got out the front looking for her wader. Upon finding it, she began to turn it upside down. Don was hollering, "Don't do that," but it was too late. His illegal clams spilled everywhere. Mary had a good nose, and it didn't take her long to smell wine. Everybody was trying to find their shovels, waders, buckets of clams, jackets, etc. What a drunken commotion. Mary was laughing and shaking her head.

One couple had a gooood recipe for clams. Even I didn't mind them. They had four-wheelers, and we rode with them sometimes. They had a dog named Candy. Candy was very stiff and sore after being rolled out the back of their camper when he took a corner too fast. Candy found her young legs when she ventured into the trees and came eyeball-to-eyeball with mama moose and baby.

Candy on 4 wheeler

NOVICE CLAMMERS

WHILE CLAMMING, MARY and I were sitting watching the two men. Someone said something to us, and when I looked up, I was astonished to see a young couple in full motorcycle regalia—black leather, scarves, tattoos. She said, "Would you take our picture? We are from Florida, and we want to prove to our friends that we were here and actually did it." I was afraid to ask what they had done. She said they were clamming. *Okay, I can handle that, but in that outfit?* I knew I had to keep from looking at Mary because I would have lost it. They proceeded to tell us they only wanted enough clams for dinner, so would we take a picture of them and their four clams? No, we did not explain to them about their four clams and dinner.

CLEANUP

BILL AND DON have gone clamming by themselves, which means I have a chance to clean up the motor home. That means I could straighten up somewhat, but first I have to do two canners and the barbie, then pick the salmon off the barbequed bones and get it ready for the third canner. That will be six canner loads in two days.

Don has figured we have a thousand pounds of salmon that the three of us have caught in the time we have been here. Bill has caught sixty-seven; Don, sixty-eight; and I, fifty-eight. This is reds only. Don was so tired last night he had leg cramps all night. We are now at the point we call "that way!" That means my fingernails and teeth are the color of salmon. All our clothes and towels are full of fish blood and gore. Smoke from the barbie and smoker is everywhere. I smell of salmon, mosquito spray, and deep heat. We are having salmon omelets, salmon off the barbie for lunch, and salmon steaks for dinner. Mary is beginning to rebel.

HOMER TO HEAL

WE WERE IN Homer laying back, healing. My fingers were so cut up I handled things gingerly. Don had two very bad cuts. Our hands were getting to the place where we could hold a fishing rod again, so we were ready to go. I spoke too soon.

We had moved to Ninilchik on the Cook Inlet. We fully intended to kick back and enjoy the view. Mary and I took our chairs and went out to the berm and sat enjoying the view. In a strangled voice, Mary shouted, "Who is that over there digging for clams?" Oh no! Not again! Those two were out there digging like backhoes. There were some blue words being said by two old women. We tried to ignore that they were dug in and were not just doing a couple of clams for fun. They were at it big time. Oh well. My hands had healed.

WILDLIFE

Mama and Baby

DON AND I put on our waders to cross the stream to take pictures of the fishing area. After you cross the stream, you walk on a narrow path through high growth just above the water. On your right, there is thirty yards and then the trees. We had made about twenty yards when mama moose and her baby crossed the water in front of us. We froze. There were two Alaskan men in front of us, and they froze, whispering, "Don't move!" Mama used her nose to abruptly send the baby into the trees and safety. Mama remained frozen, her hackles up, ears back. I thought, *We are dead!* After what seemed like an hour with no warning, Mama came boiling out of the water straight at us. The two men turned on a dime and ran over us to get away. I didn't know a sixty-six-year-old fat woman could run that fast, and Don, with his sore foot, did pretty well also. Mama turned back to her baby, laughing at us while we hyperventilated.

BIRDS

WE WOKE UP this beautiful morning to the sound of little pitter-patters of birds running around on the roof of the RV. That was common, but there was another sound added that was not so familiar. I looked out the window. The little buggers were jumping off the RV roof and sliding down the awning! I was afraid their little toes would tear the awning, so I made the mistake of opening the backdoor and hitting the awning a good whack. Well, it seems I frightened the little darlings, and they did you know what on the awning. We had planned on going into town, but that was delayed some while we got you know what off the awning.

The birds were back this morning. I hollered out the window, afraid to hit the awning again. One of them hung on to the frame and stuck his head under the awning, trying to find where the noise was coming from. When I hollered again, it startled him, and he lost his balance, turning upside down. But his tail caught on the awning, and he fell. Who needs TV?

MOOSE

ONE DAY, A moose tried to swim in the river. He missed the only spot he could make it up the bank, so he recrossed the river and rested. Then he went up the river about twenty yards and tried it again. This time he hit it dead on. How did he know how to do that?

BABY BEAR

LAST NIGHT, A baby bear walked right through camp. We all jumped and grabbed cameras. The fact that I was barefoot and in my nightie didn't even register.

PIT BULL

WE TOOK A rest from clamming and went down the beach on our ATVs. There was a harbor at Ninilchik that was full of Russian-owned fishing ships that we liked to watch. There was a young pit bull running around that belonged to the owner of the cannery. I played with him until he suddenly crouched low to the ground. I looked up to see a woman getting out of a pickup truck with a small dog. I looked down to see hackles raised and ears back. I screamed at the woman, and she saw him coming, so she tried to get back into the truck. She threw her dog, but she didn't make it. The pit bull hit her on the side. She whacked him and made it in. I went to the owner and told him what had happened. He didn't say anything, just put his dog on a leash.

EAGLE

Eagles Snoring

MY FINGERS TREMBLED as I reached for the glistening coal-black feathers. Roy, the man in charge, encouraged me, "It's okay! Try not to touch his skin—just the feathers." I had never been so close to such a magnificent creature. True, he didn't look like much at the moment, trussed up like a chicken. Since eagles receive all their input through their eyes, he was not aware of the public fuss over him. In fact, he was snoring with his head on his handler's shoulder. Judy had devoted a year of her life to bring him to this point.

More Eagles

This beautiful eagle was about to be set free. Judy had fed him, had soothed him when he chaffed at being imprisoned, and had given him his medicine. This creature should never be imprisoned, but it had been for his own good. He had flown into electric wires and burned one wing. When you see an eagle high overhead, you cannot mistake him for anything else. He should be soaring magnificently over everything—free, incomparable. Eagles are never seen in flocks as they soar, representing strength, stature, and freedom.

Roy explained to those of us privileged enough to be there, "We have tagged Ramsey so if he can't make it across the channel or if he lands on the island's beach, we can find him. I would appreciate it if you would stay where you are and don't make a sudden movement or make a sound when his hood is removed." Roy said quietly to Judy, "Let's get you positioned."

They moved alone closer to the edge of the bluff. With silent communication, Roy took hold of the Velcro-closed body covering. As he pulled it apart, Judy curled her chest away from the eagle's back. The covering fell away, freeing his wings. Roy looked at Judy, and she nodded. He carefully removed the leather coverings on the talons. Judy's arms were along Ramsey's legs, and her hands clasped the back of his feet. Now Judy moved to the edge of the bluff. When she nodded, Roy untied the hood.

Again he looked at Judy. Through her tears she nodded, and they counted to three together. Roy whipped the hood off as Judy gave a mighty heave. The surprised eagle took one mighty swoop of his fully extended wings. It gave him some lift, and then he worked hard to maintain it. His weakened body couldn't hold the altitude, and he began a slow descent to the water. We released a combined groan, our body language trying to help him. He was about twenty feet from the water when his timing returned. Gracefully, he settled on the top of a snag, disdainfully ignoring our emotional cheers.

WHALES

THE SHARP FRESH wind split around me as I searched the horizon for whales. The ferry rocked soothingly under me as I stood at the bow.

Silence allowed the talking wind to whisper and shout. The glorious sun was lowering, creating a lighting effect that squeezed the gold into red trim accenting the horizon. This helped me spot the small puffs of vapor dotting the horizon. Whales! Lots of whales! The ferry captain was heading for them, hoping to get to them before dark.

As we watched for more telltale puffs, a loud expelled push of air erupted directly below me. A foul stench passed by me as I looked down, searching. Two large whales rolled in the bows' wake. They played with us for a long time. An excited crowd now stood outside with an assortment of cameras. As the two left us, a pod of Dahl dolphins joined our wake. They flew below us sailing through the air, their black and white orca markings glistening. They would dive and slide out of the wave in another flight of fancy.

When I looked up, I realized we were close to the spot where we had seen the gray whales' puffs. Suddenly the captain announced, "Whale to the starboard!" There they were. Just as I found them, one of them breached, his fluke straight up as he dove over. What a thrill. Then two more leaped out of the water, showing their entire bodies. We were escorted by whales the entire way to Prince of Wales Island from Ketchikan. Their antics delighted us as they turned in spirals in the water, leaped, dove, and rolled as if they knew their job was to entertain the tourists.

MORE BIRDS

HUNDREDS OF VARIOUS kinds of birds meet in the morning, chasing one another from one end of the bay to the other. They follow in a single file that breaks only on the curves. The leader dives into the mist, exploding a hole for the others to follow. Passing through the invisible barrier, they would disappear to burst into sight at an unexpected place.

Misty broken outlines of boats would gradually become whole as the sun burned off the fog. Crawling down the bluff, we see fish jumping, waiting for us. At the end of the day, we walk down the road to see bears feasting on dead pinks. They are so intent on fattening up for the coming winter they pay us no heed. We watch them sniff the carcass for eggs. When they find a female, they rip open the abdominal area and suck the eggs out. Leaving the rest of the body, they go to the next. They are already fat and sleek.

MORE MAMA MOOSE

SITTING ON OUR ATVs on a bluff outside of Sutton, the wind tore at our clothes. It was a clear day, but cold. Over the edge of the bluff was a small stream with a gradual incline on the other side. We were looking for wildlife, not paying attention, which can be deadly. Loud scrambling sounds suddenly came at us from behind. Bill and I whirled to see mama moose charging down the bluff behind us. We had no weapons and reacted quickly with the only thing we could do. We got off the ATVs and crouched behind them. Then I saw her take a quick glance behind her, and sure enough, a small replica was trying his best to keep up. Rocks were flying in every direction. His little legs were wobbly, but gravity forced him downward fast.

When mama got on the flat, she charged right at us. I crouched all the way down on the ground behind my vehicle. At the last minute, she swerved and flew over the bluff without looking. Baby was right behind her. We ran to the edge of the bluff to watch if they made it when the truth of the situation hit me. I whirled around again, and then it hit Bill as he also whirled. There was a grizzly following the moose. He wanted that baby.

Instead of going by us, he went over the edge about forty yards from us. Then we watched without fear for ourselves. Mama had taken baby down the middle of the stream for quite a ways, which was difficult for Baby. Then she shoved him out and up the other side. There was thick brush that helped her. The bear was one hundred yards behind, and we lost sight of them all in the brush. We never knew the outcome, but we knew the odds were for the bear.

FISHING IN ALASKA

F ISHING IN ALASKA is strange when it is your first time. You see, the sun doesn't set. Our first day fishing, a man next to us asked his friend what time it was, and the friend answered, "Twelve thirty." Huh! It looked like four in the afternoon. We quickly quit and went to bed. I had to cover the windows with huge towels. That isn't the whole of it. The sun doesn't come up in the east or go down in the west. Because the sun is at the top of the earth, the sun comes up in the north and goes down in the north. It does a little dip at the North Pole, and that is it. This also causes the temperature during the daytime to be warm because the air and ground do not have a chance to cool off.

SOLDOTNA REDS

WE HAD PLANNED a quiet day of laundry and dinner. After laundry, we came back, and holy heck had broken loose. The reds were running. They are small and fighters. We forgot everything else, and things began to fly. Waders, poles, and everything had to be gotten out of their hiding places. We ran down and got in line. I cast out, and one hit. He flew seven feet in the air, ran around me three times, over Bill's line, and finally, he settled down enough to be netted. In fifteen minutes, I had my other two, so I became the net lady.

There were ten people with fish on all hollering for a net. A Russian fellow who didn't speak English had one on, so I netted it for him. John yelled, "Get down here with that net!" I yelled back, "I'm getting kissed by a Russian, don't bother me." John yelled, "That's my net. Forget the Russian!" Fish were flying everywhere. An older man yelled, and when I looked, the fish had yanked the pole out of his hand. Somebody cast out and got it, fish and all. One of the Russians fell in and had to be rescued. There were nine of us, and we all had our limits within an hour, and it took that long because we were laughing and carrying on so.

Bill got up at five to go fishing and made the mistake of waking me up. I got up at seven and joined him. He had one fish, and I proceeded to start hooking them. I must have had over twenty hookups that got off. I had three snagged, and then I got my third one. I must have been in a good spot. The man next to me was standing back, and I asked him if I was in his way. He said no, he was watching my technique. It took me quite a while to stop laughing. A man standing on the platform was watching me when I hooked one, yelling, "Fish on," then "Fish off" when he slacked, then "Fish on" when he pulled, then "Fish off" when he got away. The man was rolling with laughter by this time.

We did our first canner last night. It takes a time or two to get the bugs out. We got everything set up, and Bill left. Just after that, there was a huge bang, and I thought I was dead. When I realized I was okay and the canner was okay, I went around the RV to see what had exploded. It was Bill outside with the fly swatter killing mosquitoes against the RV.

A young man from Pennsylvania was fishing next to me, and he caught a big one. There was no net available, so he brought his up on the branches. The fish got off, so he made a grab for him. He got him, struggling, and lifted him triumphantly only to find he had hold of a fish he had already caught on the stringer. I tripped over a rock and went down but popped up so fast I didn't get wet.

After catching our limit for the day, we will go through the process. To do the smoker, we first catch them, clean them, fillet them, put them in brine overnight, cut them into little pieces, dry them, put pepper on, and then finally smoke them. After eight hours, we take them out and can them. If they are barbied, we put them in brine, then barbie. Next we pick it off the bones and finally can them. The fish we do raw we just can.

Yesterday when fishing, Bill was putting my sixth and last fish on the stringer when it slipped through his fingers. All six fish were floating down the river. Bill had the thought that if he lost my fish, he was dead anyway, so he risked drowning and dove for them. He got the stringer, but he was a wet puppy!

The first day at Soldotna, we were standing in the river fishing when a woman's voice shouted, "Oh no! I know you!" Bill looked and saw Linda, the woman that caused his lip to be split last year. She met a man last year, and they were married and now on their honeymoon. Steve, her husband, was fishing next to Bill when he hooked into a big one. The fish came flying out of the water, and it caught Bill in the cheek. He was so startled he went over backward and got wet. Now even his beard is fishy. Linda had needed help with a fish the year before. Bill netted her fish, and with his face over the net, the line came loose and the sinker hit him in the mouth.

When coming back up from fishing, Mary and I noticed that a lot of the rigs had their TV antennas up! We looked at each other. *Are we doing something wrong?* The men hollered at us to hurry up, so we went back and told them everybody else was watching TV. We decided to put up our antennas even though we don't have TVs just so everybody would think we were bored with fishing too and were inside with nothing to do. It's not funny when we are inside with the sweat dripping; it is so hot from the canner. Bill's face was so red from the heat. Oh well, we will feel sorry for those people when we are enjoying our salmon during the winter.

FISHING ENTERTAINMENT

IF THE FISHING is slow, there is always something to entertain you. A couple came down to the river who had never fished before. Hazel was saying, "Honey, my line is too long. Honey, how do I know if I catch one, etc." Well, somebody upriver caught one, and she didn't know it. When it exploded at her stomach, she screamed and fell in the water. She kept screaming, "The fish is biting me!" When she got up, she was soaked but good-natured. I explained that when someone shouts "Fish on," she should step back and reel in. She now was hollering at Honey for not telling her. Bill told her if she would do it again, he would set up chairs on the platform and charge admission and she could have half. She was able to laugh with the rest of us.

PEOPLE YOU MEET

WHILE FISHING FOR silvers at Willow, we had to walk quite a ways to get to flowing water. We figured we would be alone when we got to our spot. As we were walking through the riverbed, we turned a bend, and there was a boat right in the sweetest spot. The fellow inside had rigged a shade with a raggedy towel. He was dressed slovenly and was unkempt. He was eating Wal-Mart cookies and fishing over the side. "Hello!" he said. "Come on in and put your line right there. Want a cookie?" I put my line where he had told me, and *wham!* A silver. "See what I mean?"

We caught more and talked. He told us he had caught a silver but didn't want him. He sprung out of the boat and said, "I know what we'll do with him!" He dug out a rusted grate and piled four rocks in the sand. When he had the rocks just right, he carefully placed the grate on top. Starting a fire, he went back to fishing until the embers were just right, then he placed the fish on top. While we fished, it cooked. I did worry a little about the bear, but we could always jump into the boat, I guess. When the fish was done, we ate what we wanted. For some reason, it tasted better than the fish I cooked with all the amenities.

For the rest of the day we talked and ate on the fish when we felt like it. When we told Scott we were going to head back, he insisted on taking us in his boat, which he did. It turned out Scott was a brilliant, educated man, but you wouldn't have guessed it from his appearance—unkempt beard and Alaskan slang. We fished with Scott for two or three days.

FISHING DOG

WHILE FISHING AT Willow for our kings, it was again combat fishing. One fellow showed up in his chest waders, fishing pole, and his miniature pincher tucked into his chest waders. He had hitchhiked that way to get there. When fishing, he would put the dog down. The dog was walking back to the line of fishermen when a man whipped his line back to cast. It caught the dog, who yelped as he went flying through the air, landing in the water. He quickly swam ashore whimpering. The man apologized profusely, but the owner just laughed and said, "That's okay. I was going to get his ears pierced anyway."

Alaskan Kenai Combat Fishing

FISHING FAMILIES

ALASKAN CHILDREN GROW up self-sufficient. They have to be. While Mom and Dad fish, the kids are into dirt mixed with fish, blood, and gore. If they fall or get hurt, Mom yells, "Take care of it yourself!" If it is a scream that sounds serious, Mom looks over her shoulder.

One young mother had her toddler in a full winter suit with a harness over that. The harness was tied to a tree, and the kid was left on her own until Mom got her king salmon for the day. In the meantime, if the kid fell, tough. Dogs licked her; she ate dirt or anything else in reach. Oh well, she seemed healthy and happy.

Kids approach strangers as friends and can entertain themselves. One of the three-year-olds came up to where Bill was sitting. With blond curls and blue eyes, she said, "What is your name?" Bill told her, and then she wanted him to write it in the dirt, and she gave him a stick. He did so, and she spent a long time copying it. Another little whipper with no teeth got down where the fishermen were, and Bill told him he better get back, and he answered, "If I get hurt, it is my fault!" The beach where you stand to fish is about ten feet and then a sharp bank about five feet high where the kids and watchers stand. This kid's dad didn't break stride; he just turned around and, with one hand, threw the kid up where he was supposed to be. The kid landed on his feet, and his dad went on fishing without a comment.

Fishing Families

KING SALMON

T HE SURPRISE JOLT ripped at my joints. I hung on to the fishing rod, now bent double, screaming, "Fish on!" Immediately thirty men to my right and twenty to my left pulled their lines in, allowing me to work my king salmon. He took off downstream, my line screaming. I knew better than to try and stop him. *Don't spool me*, I thought. I waited, my elbows burning. He slowed, I puffed. He came jerking, fighting. I got him ten feet closer when he took off again. Feet slipping in the mud, he inched me downstream instead of me pulling him upstream. I saw men around me rolling their eyes as I struggled, needing all my strength. I imagined them thinking, "Fat old lady is going to take all day." This is called combat fishing—shoulder to shoulder—and while someone is working a fish, no one else can fish.

Bill approached me. "Should I tighten your drag?" Tersely I snapped, "Don't touch it!" I had watched the Alaskans carefully before stepping into a spot. It was my first time, and I wanted to get it right. I needed all I had learned.

Just as I thought I had outlasted him, he would take off again. It had been twenty minutes. Groans! He rested. I rested. The swift-moving river glistened around him, rippling. My breath was coming hard and fast. The cold midnight air stabbed at me as I gathered myself for one last effort. I was making headway, but my arms were dead. Downstream, a cry rang out, "Snagged!" The toothless Alaskan who had been helping me shouted back, "Land him anyway!"

I reached down for all the reserved strength I had. He inched away from the shore downstream. He was tiring. His tugs were less violent. Now he was in the mainstream of the river again. I kept the tip down in the water and pulled hard. He came toward me without restraint. My toothless friend grabbed a net. Everyone moved as one toward the river in anticipation of fish landed. Not quite yet. He gave one last tug trying to run, but I held on. He came in.

57 lb King Salmon
My first

The man stepped toward him with the net, and with one strong stab, he was landed. The man hollered for all to hear, "I can't lift him, and he's not snagged!" Someone helped him, and my adversary lay before me. He was huge, almost completely red and fifty-seven pounds. A chorus of oohs and ahs, well dones, and wows came from my new partners as they stepped back to the river. My friend said to me quietly, just for me, "Well done!" He sliced a sliver of raw flesh and handed it to me. I ate the strip, savoring the honor. This is the highest respect bestowed on an Alaskan fisherman for your first fish.

PS: The next day, I was having trouble getting up the muddy bank when a young man offered his hand to help. I said to him, "Do you stand around all day just to help old ladies up the bank?" He answered, "Don't give me that. I was here yesterday when you landed that king."

WILLOW CREEK

WE SETTLED INTO our favorite campground and quickly changed into our chest waders. We took our fishing gear and waded across the shallow creek. Up the muddy bank and through the tall grass, we made our way to the river. This river emptied into a large, fast-moving river. We fished for five days, and then the rain started. After four days of rain, when we crossed the shallow creek, it wasn't so shallow. Going through the tall grass heightened your senses when you knew a bear was in the undergrowth somewhere.

We fished all day in the rain. Bill had brought along a fly-fishing pole just to try it for the first time. I got my line tangled, so my hero had me hold the fly pole while he untangled mine. I decided to try this strange contraption and managed to get the line out when *wham!* A fish hit. I frantically tried to reel him in, shouting, "How do I use this thing?" Bill was laughing so hard he couldn't do anything but shout, "Hold on to the line!" I thought about which I wanted more, my hand or the fish, but I grabbed the line with my hand, and the jerking became more personal. For the life of me, I couldn't figure out how to bring the fish in, so I started to back up until I was on the edge of the river. The fish was still on as I dragged him up on shore. By this time, Bill could help. Bill cleaned all the fish and threw the remains in the river so the bears would not be attracted. We packed the steaks in ziplocks and put them in a backpack that Bill carried and then headed back.

When we got to the creek, I knew I was in trouble. Bill got down the muddy bank easily. I skidded down. When I got into the water, it quickly edged up to the top of my chest waders. I yelped, and Bill turned around to see my predicament. He reached out his long arm, grabbed my shoulder strap, and waded me across. We left for another area the next day.

WHAT ARE FRIENDS FOR?

OUR FIRST DAY back at Willow, Bill couldn't wait to get fishing. He grabbed his pole and was gone. After a short nap, Don followed. Don came back first with three pinks, looking sheepish. He explained the fishing was so good there was a bunch of kids on the bank. His first thought had been, "Oh no, I am going to have fishhooks everywhere." It turned out he didn't have to worry about the kids. Some bearded old guy got him in the crotch. Bill broke up, so I knew who the old guy was. Don went on, "Ya, I told Bill, 'Come here and get this hook out of my crotch. I can't see it.' Bill said, 'I'd rather cut your pants. They have holes in them anyway. I am not going to get down on my hands and knees and dig around in your crotch!'"

MORE FISH DOG

Rosie Fishing

VALDEZ SILVERS WERE running hard. Tom and his Jack Russell female dog named Rosie were in their element. Rosie would wait trembling with anticipation, her toes just touching the edge of the water. If Tom took too long to hook into one, Rosie would give an impatient ruff.

Once Tom did hook a silver, she became a leaping, barking, squealing, screaming furball until it was close enough to shore for her to reach with her teeth without drowning. Then the poor hapless fish was shaken side to side with such force fish gunk would spray around her head in a necklace of sparkles. When she was sure she had taken care of the problem, she would drag the fish ashore where Tom would try to talk her out of it. While Rosie had been doing her job, she had been standing in thousands of dead pinks, which gave off an odor a skunk would run from. The time Tom spent catching his limit of six was enough to reduce Rosie to the raunchiest fish dog in Valdez. Poor Rosie was forced to ride in the back of the pickup with the fish.

The following day, there was Tom and Rosie back at it, but I noticed Rosie was a trembling ball of subdued excitement laying with her back to the water on Tom's sweatshirt. I asked Tom why Rosie wasn't entertaining the beach. Tom laughed and said it had taken him an hour to bathe her well enough to make her acceptable to join him in bed. Poor Rosie. Shaking like a leaf, she restrained herself with obvious effort whenever Tom hooked a fish. Once when she couldn't stand it anymore, she made a dash into the water. Tom whirled and shouted, "Bath!" And Rosie whirled for the beach so fast she stumbled. She spent the rest of the afternoon curled up on the ground in turn growling and whining with her shaking rear end facing the water, showing disgust with the world.

SEAL

Bill fighting a Seal

O N A BEAUTIFUL slow fishing day in Valdez, Bill was trying to catch his silver limit. He threw his line in the water and slowly reeled in. Suddenly, the beauty of Valdez Bay disappeared from view as water splashed and a huge silver leaped five feet out of the water close to shore. Bill fought him as he ran until he suddenly seemed to try a new tactic. The line stopped jerking, and he began a slow, even retreat. Bill thought, *This fish isn't that big! Why can't I stop him?* He tried everything. He put his pole tip in the water, turned his pole on its side, but nothing worked. His line steadily made its way out into the bay. Slowly, a dark sleek head began to emerge. A seal! The seal had Bill's fish in its mouth, and Bill's lure flashed in the salmon's mouth.

When the seal got a look at Bill, he glared at him and at the people now pointing and laughing. The seal was so shocked he dropped the fish. Bill began to reel frantically before the seal could recover, but he was not quick enough. The seal grabbed the fish again, and Bill bent double with the weight.

Bill was sure the fish was so traumatized by this time he doubted the fish cared who won. The fight was on. The seal and Bill glared at one another. Bill would gain a few yards, and then the seal would bear down, and out the poor fish would go. Working hard, Bill pulled the seal within fifteen yards ashore. With a fish in his mouth, the seal couldn't swim backward with force. It was finally more than he could take. He let go. The people on the beach erupted in cheers along with the Alyeska workers who had stopped on the road to watch. Bill held the wounded fish high and took a bow as the seal slunk away.

CLEAN

THIS KIND OF life truly is not for everyone. Just to get my hair washed into something that does not resemble fish muck is a challenge. Then there are my hands. After handling raw fish, I wash and then disinfect so that hopefully my hands will stay attached to my arms. Then there are my fingernails, which are stained with and full of marinade. This is what I wash my hair with, and I wonder why I am going bald! But when those fifteen pounders are jumping on your line, you forget clean.

ONLY IN ALASKA

A FRIEND'S DESCRIPTION OF a weekend fishing. They flew with a pilot friend to a small lake to fish for silvers. They landed on the lake fine and had a great weekend. When it came time to leave, she realized the lake was too small to take off from, especially with tall trees surrounding it. The pilot was busy tying the back of the plane to a tree with a rope. He then gunned the engine as high as it would crank up, reaching out the door with a machete, and gave the rope a good whack. They slingshot over the trees, brushing them as they went by.

Living next to our friend John is Doc. Doc has a small typical Alaskan plane. One day, John heard a strange plane noise and went to investigate. Doc had taken off without removing a chock on one side. He was now flying in a very low circle, getting lower with each pass. He finally ended up in the small creek with only a bump on his head. Once, he went hunting in his plane to a remote area. He was told to pee on his tires so the raccoons wouldn't tear them up, but he just laughed. When he got back to his plane, the raccoons had chewed his tires badly enough he didn't think he could take off. He got out the Alaskan's best friend—duct tape. He managed to take off to discover he had left his gun on the bank of the lake. When he went back, the raccoons had chewed the stock of his gun. Upon landing, his tires gave out completely, but the plane was okay.

John went up with him once but never again. He said there was not one thing on the plane that worked and everything was held together with duct tape. Doc can't fly right now because a moose ate his ailerons during the winter.

ALASKAN GARDEN

OUR FRIEND JOHN had a new weeder for his garden. It was a box with no bottom and with chicken wire on two sides. When I got closer, I could see there were two chickens in the box. John explained they had two jobs, and when they had accomplished those two jobs, he rewarded them. The first job was to eat the weeds, and the second was to get rid of the weeds from the other end, as he put it. When they had fertilized his garden, he rewarded them by moving the box.

ABBY'S MOOSE

Abby's Moose

ONE BALMY DAY, John was working in his wonderful garden. He had been bending over for a long time, so when he heard his dog, Abby, approach, he stood to stretch his back. When he did so, his head hit something rather hard. When he was completely upright, he was face-to-face with a moose. John screamed, which frightened the moose. Abby was frightened and began barking. Kathy came out to find out what on earth was going on. John screamed, "Abby brought a moose home to play with."

ANOTHER JOHN'S MOOSE

JOHN AND KATHY were sleeping soundly when it sounded like something was pulling the roof off. John jumped up and remembered to put on shoes before going out in the snow. When he rounded the house, a moose was hung up in his Christmas lights, yanking and pulling. The trouble was they were attached to the roof. The roof was being pulled off.

ANOTHER FAT OLD LADY STORY

WHILE IN VALDEZ, Bill went to the beach to hunt for lures, leaving me in my nightie trying to catch up on my sleep. *Wham!* A wind shear hit that shook the RV. Our awning was out. I leaped out of bed and went out to grab the pole of the awning just as our neighbor Kenny lost his awning. The wind was picking up the awning and slamming it back down again. I managed to get a good hold on one corner and hung on. Now the wind was picking up my large heft and the awning. When there was a lull, I got the smoker off the Coleman stove and tied the awning to a pail full of water. It was at this juncture that I realized I was still in my nightie. The good part was it was a long flannel nightie; otherwise, the world would have been treated to a nude old fat lady dangling from an awning.

ANOTHER ONE

L HAD ON my chest waders, fishing far from civilization. I had to go to the bathroom, so I went into the woods like everybody else. I was so proud of myself until I finished dressing and realized I had peed on my straps. Oh well, maybe next time.

PICKING BERRIES

D ON, MARY, BILL, and I had pulled over into a rest area between Palmer and Glennallen to pick berries. Mary and I were done and back at the RV talking. We were watching out the front window for a sign of our men. Suddenly, from across the road out of the trees came a bear on his way to his favorite berry patch. I jumped out of the RV and screamed at the men. No reaction. I got closer and screamed again. Finally, Mary joined me. A head popped up. We screamed, "Bear!" The head disappeared. Mary and I figured if they didn't care, why should we?

LAUNDROMATS

DIRTY HAIR SPREAD in greasy clumps over the shoulders of a filthy shirt. The young man wearing the shirt opened the door briskly and headed straight for his favorite washer. Slinging his backpack onto the floor, he emptied dirty clothes into the washer. Encrusted jeans, underwear, shirts, and a jacket were squeezed in. Then he stripped off his shirt and added that to the mess. Next, his shoes came off and were stuffed into the backpack. Socks a skunk would like to mate with were carefully peeled off and added. He then headed for the shower and reappeared with his underwear in hand. The soap dispenser he used, saving a little for the shower. After starting the machine, he again headed for the shower.

Quite a while later, he came through the door another person. He had obviously washed his pants in the shower as they were sopping wet. His long hair now glistened and curled, hanging loose. As he walked by me, I said, "Do you know if there is a dryer better than the others?" Immediately his face retreated. He lowered his empty gray eyes and said shyly, "Yes, ma'am. Follow me." He took me to the last dryer and then gave me a long lesson on how to use it to get the most out of it. Trying to draw him out of his shell, I added, "I am impressed with your knowledge. I've never done this before." With that he showed me each dryer and told me what to look for.

He excused himself, took a pair of mostly dry jeans out of the dryer, and headed for the shower. He returned with the jeans he had had on and put them in the dryer. "You have quite a system," I told him. He explained, never once looking me in the eye, "I come in from the bush once a month to wash and get the supplies I need." We visited while his clothes finished drying. I asked if he needed help getting out the door. He didn't answer, just nodded for me to follow him outside. He turned, looking directly into my eyes with an open face for the first time. "Ma'am, don't romanticize my way of life or envy me. I'm wanted outside for killing my father." He turned and was gone.

ALLISON POINT

ALLISON POINT IN Valdez is one of our favorite places to camp while we fish. The road to Alyeska and the end of the pipeline ends just beyond Allison Point. After 9/11, everything changed. Each evening, a tough-looking guy in a uniform would walk behind the RVs parked there with a camera and film the RVs and the license plates. Buoys have been placed in the water around the Alyeska area. If a boat is unlucky enough to cross that line even slightly, there is no warning. Immediately there is a Coast Guard boat there, and there is a huge fine with a jail sentence.

A new entrance to Alyeska has been built. It crosses the entire road, and no one is allowed in. If a car or fisherman approaches too closely, you are warned, and you better stop. If you don't understand and you get too close, guns are drawn. Ships that carry the oil out are now escorted by more than one boat. It is possible to fish without being distracted by all the care to protect the oil line, but it can get interesting.

PALMER PARADE

Star's of the Palmer Parade

ONE YEAR, WE were lucky enough to be in Palmer when they had their spring parade. But this parade was quite different from what we were used to. Remember, we come from LA, where there is a parade called the Rose Parade. In the Palmer parade, we heard cheering from the audience, so we waited excitedly to see what was so special. A third of the parade was weiner dogs of all kinds. There were even puppies in wagons. They were decorated in all kinds of outlandish attire.

Following the short-legged stars, there were several teenagers on skateboards being pulled by sled dogs. They were moving so fast they would fly by the rest of the parade and then around to the back and do it all over again. If a local wished to just get in the parade and walk, they were welcome. Oh, for the joys of a small town.

YUKON AND PORCUPINE RIVERS

Bill twirling stick over head to fend off nesting bird

O NE YEAR, WE were lucky enough to take a boat trip from Fort Yukon to Old Crow. The boat was quite small. Our friends Sharon and Johnny, Johnny's cousin, and the man driving the boat made for a crowded boat, but we didn't care. While in Fort Yukon, we observed that most of the young native people were drunk along with most of the adults. When the tourists were flown in for a bus trip around Fort Yukon, they would scour the town and put all the people who were drunk out of sight. We finally were ready and we left Fort Yukon.

On the first day, we had to stop for a bathroom break. Sharon was a city gal and had never encountered this kind of restroom. The driver pulled over to the bank and gave each of us a long stick. There was a bird that was nesting and would attack, so the stick was to be swung around our heads to protect us from being pecked. Sharon left and went on the other side of a downed tree. It didn't take long for her screams to alert us she was in trouble. I ran to her, but she seemed okay. She was screaming her head off about her butt. It seems she had trouble coordinating swinging the branch around her head and trying to swat the mosquitoes who were feasting on her bare bottom. That didn't start the day off too well.

We stopped for the night at a cabin Johnny's cousin knew. Before we were allowed out of the boat, they went with a bear rifle to check the area. When everything seemed clear of bears, we carried our supplies inside. I didn't like the deep, long bear claw marks on the door but didn't point this out to Sharon. When inside, Sharon and I started to get something to eat. Sharon headed right for the sink and tried to turn on the water. Whoops! That didn't work. Sharon loudly wanted to know how we were going to get dinner without water. We managed.

The next day was beautiful. Bears would be on the beach not frightened of these strange-looking swimmers. We made it to Old Crow and immediately we realized this was a whole different ball game. No one was drunk or on drugs. The teenagers were all in school. Of course, we were in Canada. A Mountie was assigned to the town and stayed there, but he was not in charge of the law.

The elders were holding court when we arrived because someone had been caught with a bottle of beer. We stayed with Johnny's mother and his brother, Ernie. We were invited to a potlatch and learned to eat strange food and even Eskimo ice cream. Don't try it. After a couple of days, we sadly left. We were able to see where the gold miners had traveled and learned much of the history of the area. It was quite beautiful being in the wilderness without sound or sign of civilization.

When we returned to Fort Yukon, we took the same boat back to Circle, where our RVs were waiting. On the trip, Bill and I noticed the gas was in an open barrel. We were shocked as gas spilled over onto everything including the motor. When we arrived close to Circle, I noticed Bill get up and go back to sit by the driver. I panicked slightly when I saw Bill pumping the bulb to get gas into the engine. Yes, we were going to run out of gas before we made it to Circle. The Yukon is not a forgiving river. Bill was giving me the look to keep quiet, which I did. Exactly as the boat scraped against the shore, we ran out of gas. No one ever knew.

Boat
6 of us traveled up to Old Crow

KNIVES SHARPENED

W E FOLLOWED DON'S rig down the narrow road to Seward. Along the way, signs informed us we could sharpen our knives two miles ahead. Mary let us know over the CB that Don was pulling off to take advantage of the offer. We pulled over, and Bill got out his knives. It turned out to be a water grinding wheel, and the men went to work. As Mary stood there watching, a light went on. She turned to me with a twinkle in her eye. "You know, my nails are in sad shape. I think I'll use this huge fingernail file." Laughing, we placed our nails against the grinding wheel and watched our nails fly away.

When we left Seward, we camped in a beautiful state campground with lupine surrounding the motor home. Mary and I went for a walk around the campground. A woman was getting out of her huge, expensive, polished RV. The woman said hello, so we stopped and visited. I knew we were in trouble as I studied her. She had on tan linen slacks, a rose silk blouse, rose slippers, two huge diamonds on her fingers matching what was in her ears. Every clean hair was in place, and the worst thing of all, she had on makeup. The conversation turned to Alaska. Mary asked, "How do you like Alaska?" The woman responded, "I like it fine, but I'm having a devil of a time finding a place to get my nails done."

Mary and I actually made it back to the RV before we disgraced ourselves.

VALDEZ

Teenage Grizzly escaping capture

D EEP ASLEEP, RIPPING, tearing sounds woke us. Bill turned the flashlight outside under the awning. A grizzly was tearing at my ATV. His bottom on my handlebars, he balanced, teetering as his sharp claws tore my seat off. Bill hollered and clapped, but he might as well have whispered. Yelling and pounding, the grizzly nonchalantly, as if we were interrupting his playtime, slid off, wandering away.

In the morning, we were examining my ATV when the grizzly strolled by us so close I could smell him. The camp host had called the police, which was overkill to us, but the police explained if the same bear kept bothering tourists, they would remove him to an island. They informed us bears liked the foam in ATV seats.

The following day, we went to town to the police station for a copy of the report for insurance purposes. We were told we couldn't have it yet because the case was still pending. The perp was still at large!

When we returned to our campsite, two black bears were sitting on our picnic table. Since we were the last ones in the campground, we were beginning to feel uncomfortable.

That night a black bear woke us, but when Bill hollered, she wandered off a ways. Since he was up, Bill headed for the bathroom. I had planned what I was going to do if we were disturbed again. There she came. She was heading for the ATVs, so I reached for my two heavy metal pan lids. I waited until she was way under the awning and let fly with a horrific crash. I had no idea lids could make a sound comparable to a gunshot. The bear went straight up about seven feet, legs thrashing. Doubled up with spasms of laughter, I heard hollering. Bill! I had forgotten he was in the bathroom. He was screaming at the top of his lungs, "What was that? Was that a gunshot? Was that you?" There was some cleaning of the bathroom required. Not much sleep that night for all the laughter. We decided to give in and let the bears have the campground, leaving two days early.

NORTHERN LIGHTS

I WOKE IN the middle of the night, and as I often do, I opened the curtain by my head. The entire sky had turned a brilliant green that was flowing and swooping. I woke Bill up. We watched the green grow dim then bright as the color drained from one area to fill another. A splash would fly across and then spill downward as paint spills, leaving trails of lighter green.

GARAGE SALES

BILL AND I love to go to garage sales in Alaska. You can find things you won't find anywhere else in the world. One summer, I bought a rifle at a garage sale. Now how do I get it across Canada? You have to get a permit and pay a fee. When you get to the border, you are supposed to show the gun and paperwork. I had left Bill alone to travel home because I had flown to Minnesota from Alaska. When Bill got to the border, he went in and declared the gun. They didn't want to see it, just the paperwork. When Bill went back in the RV, he put the gun away, and when he did, a round fell out of the chamber. That is very much against the law in Canada and means big trouble. You know who was the one who got in trouble!

NIGHTLY ROUTINE

F IRST WE TAKE down everything stacked on the upper bed. The chair, a box of extra clothes, a sack of new clothes, Snoopys, a radio, a box with cassettes, crackers, a box of books, and a container of maps. Then we start at the back and do the same thing. The box of water and our shoes are moved. Then we can get to the middle, put the bed down, and the process is started over. Things are put up on the bed empty of the mattress so we can get to the bathroom during the night. Reverse everything in the morning.

RV COOKING

L AST NIGHT I made RV Jell-O. I put canned fruit and trail mix in it. When Bill got to the nuts, he looked at it and said, "Moose turds are going too far. I want regular Jell-O." Oh well, I'll stick to ice cream.

TOGETHERNESS

ANYONE WHO HAS ever RV'd with a spouse knows you have to be good friends. Bill and I travel in a twenty-foot motor home, so we have to be especially amicable. There are things that do put a dent in all this togetherness.

One night, we were in bed reading. Bill fell asleep as I continued to read. Something caught my eye. A huge spider was crawling on my tummy toward my arm. Without a second thought, I took my book and—well, you know the rest. Living in small quarters becomes more difficult as the summer goes on with twenty-four boxes of canned salmon and fifteen pints of blueberry jam and as gifts for the family accumulate. Our togetherness became more strained when I saw Bill walking toward the RV carrying a moose rack. I guess we can sleep standing up.

BILL

I FIXED LUNCH for Bill and then went to the back of the RV to straighten up some things. I heard the strangest crunching sound. When I turned, Bill had opened up the ziplock that held my favorite piece of bark with all kinds of moss and good stuff hanging from it. When he turned, I realized he was eating it. I screamed, "What are you doing?" He answered, "I thought it was jerky!"

Another day, Bill was going to fix an omelet for breakfast. I turned just as he poured Joy soap into the pan instead of the oil.

When Bill finished breakfast, I told him he had a big chunk of butter in his beard. He told me he knew about it and he was leaving it there for a reason. Huh? Why? So the gnats would go for that and leave my forehead alone.

Bill came storming back from fishing. It was still Labor Day and gangland fishing at Valdez. There were a hundred fishing to his left and a hundred fishing to his right. The guy next to him kept looking at him, glancing, and then looking away. Bill was used to strange people in Alaska, so he paid no attention. Finally, the man yelled for everyone to hear, "I know who you are! You're Willy Nelson!" The whole line of fishermen were stretching and looking and whispering. Bill told the guy no, but he said, "That's okay. I won't tell anybody." Bill had to come back to get some peace before he tried to find someplace else to fish.

The canner was going full blast, and there was not too much room to wiggle between the table and the canner. Bill stood talking to me, and in the middle of a word, he screamed, "I'm on fire!" And when he turned, he was. His T-shirt was burning upward. I slapped it out and yanked his T-shirt off, which would be kept in the Held Hall of Fame. The only damage besides the T-shirt was some singed butt hairs.

Really? Willie Nelson?

Bill's big day in Yellowknife, Northwest Territory. We were trying to find information on his grandfather who came through that area during the gold rush. He went to the mining office. When he came back, he had his Bill smirk. I said, "You found your grandfather's mine?" And I received a blank stare. "No," he said, "look what the receptionist gave me." He had an old Snoopy clock that worked. It was fantastic. The lady receptionist found out he collected Snoopy and insisted he take it. That is the way people are up there.

Bill was recognized by people who had been in Valdez last year. He quickly became known as the expert. People came to him to ask how to rig their line, and he helped. He also was known as the Seal Stealer. Last year, he outlasted a seal in a fight for a fish.

I still had fifty hot flashes at night. So it was throw the covers off and three minutes later scramble for the covers as it was cold at night. Later, throw the covers off and three minutes—well, you get the idea. Bill said in his monotone, "Okay, I am getting up. I am turning on the lights. I am getting two clothespins. I am getting back in bed. I am clipping the covers to my ears."

Bill fell in yesterday in all the dead-pink muck. And I had to sleep with him.

FIRE

ALL OF SUMMER 2004, there was no rain. The many fires caused smoke all the way to Kodiak. Leaving in late September, we drove through smoke from fires that had been left to burn. Our throats burned and eyes teared. The rivers fed from glaciers were running because of the fast glacier melt, but the other rivers were very dry. In some places such as Willow, the salmon couldn't get upstream to spawn. They were trying to think of other ways to get the baby salmon where they belonged.

OUR FIRE

LEAVING VALDEZ, THERE is a killer of a grade. The grade is about twenty-one miles long and steep. We were hauling a trailer full of sixty boxes of canned salmon, two ATVs, and all our other paraphernalia. Our little twenty-one-foot 1976 motor home did just fine, but about a third of the way up the grade, Bill screamed, "We're on fire!" He pulled over as I grabbed the fire extinguisher.

Before we left Valdez, Bill had pulled the motor mount off to check the engine, and when he put the mount back down, he didn't notice the carpet was squinched underneath touching the manifold. The heat of the engine had ignited the carpet. Flames were licking at Bill's leg. I doused the area with the extinguisher, and we were okay. The engine or belts were not damaged. As shaken as we were, we made it up the grade and sailed on home.

LEAVING THROUGH CANADA

W E ARE CARRYING a caribou rack on the back and a bloody, hairy moose rack as a hood ornament. Since we look a little different, we made sure we would be okay to take all of these through Canada. We have made it, and nobody took anything. We are in cultural shock with all the traffic and noise, so the first thing we do when we get back outside is take Excedrin.

Unpacking

CPSIA information can be obtained at www.ICGtesting.com
Printed in the USA
LVOW081048220612

287141LV00004B/2/P